# BECOMING A BETTER PERSON

Larry Cyril and Bridger Lee Jensen

# BECOMING A BETTER PERSON

LARRY CYRIL AND BRIDGER LEE JENSEN

**Larry Cyril and Bridger Lee Jensen**
*larrycyriljensen@gmail.com*

Published by **Authors Branding**
*9620 Las Vegas Blvd S Ste E4 632*
*Las Vegas, NV 89123, USA*
*support@authorsbranding.com*
*(725) 240-6558*

*ISBN: 979-8-9896059-7-2 (paperback)*
*ISBN: 979-8-9896059-8-9 (ebook)*

# PREFACE

Whether you think you are a good person or a bad one you can become a better person. Become more joyful, happier, successful, competent and more. How do you do it? You change, you grow, you expand and evolve. Welcoming change is the key. Instead of resisting or merely accepting change you embrace it.

More than a decade ago I was invited to teach a course on becoming successful in marriage. At the end of the class one of my students helped me collect my lectures and write the book, *Becoming a Better Marriage Partner*. Now, sitting down to write this book, I realize how much my marriage book was about personal change and so we will draw heavily on it's content to write for you this book, *Becoming a Better Person*.

I am motivated to write this book because my son Bridger, who is a therapist, notices that many of his clients upon completion of their sessions do look for the best most practical ways to move forward in becoming the best person they can be. Fortunately, it came to my recollection that Decades ago, in the twentieth century, it was popular for psychology departments to offer a course on individual differences. When teaching this course in the 1960's, I used a book entitled *Stability and Change in Human Characteristics*, by Benjamin Bloom. From teaching this course I came to realize that in general, we act as if each individual is a stable material object. However, whenever much reflection is given to this question the answer is in the opposite direction. You and I and all people are found to change during the life course, during the year, during the day, and even each moment. We are constantly changing entities not stable objects?

So the pathway is open for all of us to become a better person. You will find in this short little book important streps, tips, and guiding ideas to help you become a better person. That is why I asked Bridger to coauthor this book for you.

# BECOMING A BETTER PERSON

## First Thoughts About Becoming a Better Person

Philosophers, psychologists, and behavior scientists have almost always postulated that there is something inside a person that influences the behavior of an individual person. Considersome of the names they have proposed; consciousness, awareness, self, and ego. A past President of the American Psychological Association, Albert Bandura centered his theory around the phrase, "self-sufficiency" which he defined as the capacity of the self to exert control over motivation, well-being, and personal behavior. Other psychologists refer to self-monitoring, self, self- concept, self -esteem, self-regard, self-control. Over and over the word self is used to refer to something inside the person.

The voices of existential philosophers from Kierkegaard, Heidegger, and Satre have proposed that humans must be understood in a very different way. Their famous saying "existence precedes essence" leads us to the belief that a person first exists, which is our existence, and then the person creates his/her essence. In this book I interpret this key statement in a way to present a positive, hopeful conclusion.

This statement of existence precedes essence is interpreted here as that each human begins with an existence and then each creates or develops an essence. The essence is what we become; it is us, it is our consciousness, our awareness, it is really what we are as we live each day. We create our essence from our choices, perceptions, and reactions during our everyday lived experiences.

Most people now and in the past believe that combined with the body and the mind is a spirit. Christian and most religions believe that a spirit exists as part of the person, or the person is or has a spirit. Even non-religious scholarship often refers to man's spirit. In common language we say such things as, "He has a mean spirit", "Don't break the boys spirit", and "You have a good spirit", If you believe that each person has a spirit and the spirit has an enduring eternal quality then everything you conclude about yourself and others will be different. If the spirit endures after the body, then isn't it just logical to conclude that the spirit is the central or key enduring feature of the person you are now and are always creating?

# A Person is a Body, Mind and Spirit

*The old woman was skipping, almost dancing as she flittered around the large hall. The program was over and the cleanup had begun. Her eyes beamed as she moved among those clearing the tables and visiting. She held my attention as I thought her childish actions were unbecoming of a person her age. "Who does she think she is?" "She should act her age.*

*Then suddenly, everything changed. The grandmother transformed into a little girl. I saw her in her youth. I saw within the old body a young vibrant spirit. My criticisms melted. I felt so good watching her enjoy life. I felt she was so lucky to still have a young joyful spirit. I felt I was fortunate to be able to, at that moment, see more than meets the eye.*

At that moment, the old woman was more than just a worn out body. For a slight moment her spirit was seen. This is the key to becoming a better person. It is to realize that we are more than a body. We all have a spirit or to be more correct; we are first and foremost spirits.

This, of course, is not mentioned in academic textbooks. In these books, there is one hundred percent agreement that each person is a body made of material that can, by physicists, be reduced or identified into smaller and smaller units such as protons and electrons. They may disagree about the basic units but all agree that people are reducible to some kind of matter and energy. The next area, with one hundred percent agreement, is that we have a mind. The popular belief is that the brain is the mind.

But you might, as many others, want to add a third element to the question of "What are we?" Most people now and in the past believe a spirit is combined with the body and the mind. Christianity, Judaism, Islam, and almost all religions believe that a spirit exists as part of the person, or the person is or has a spirit. Again, this belief is found in almost all religious writing. For example, nowhere is it stated more directly than in Job 32:8: "But there is a spirit in man; and the inspiration of the Almighty giveth them understanding." To become your best person possible you must understand the spirit, as well as the body, and the mind. How is this done? We will discuss this in more detail later.

# A Person is an Agent

In a class for family improvement, the following story was told:

*In a busy airport, a hurried and hungry middle age mother purchased a sack of cookies at the gift shop next to her gate. She was deep in thought and after a few minutes was surprised to see the man next to her casually take a cookie from the sack. She was astonished at his rudeness and to let him know better she also took a cookie and conspicuously ate it so he would get the idea. Feeling her space was being invaded she let him know by reaching in for another and gave him a serious look. He did not seem to mind or get the idea as he took another. His reaction was not what she intended as he just smiled and even reached for yet another. Then into her mind raced the calloused, selfish, antagonistic memory of her father, and how she had to protect herself from men like him all her life. She took another and so did he until there was only one cookie left. To add further insult he took the last cookie, broke it in half, and offered it to her. She could stand this no more and with tears, yet angry, she stood up and rushed to her gate. At the gate, she opened her purse for a tissue to wipe her eyes, and there noticed her sack of unopened cookies.*

This story can illustrate a number of human attributes. It can be an introduction to the idea that how we respond is a choice we make because we are agentic. As self-directing agents, we can choose how to respond. In the story the man, choose to respond with a smile and good feelings about sharing, even the last cookie. The woman, on the other hand, chose to see herself as a victim. Of course, there were other extenuating circumstances such as the misperception of ownership of the sack and she may have had good reasons to see the worst in men. Let us consider another true and extreme example of a man who had reason to be bitter but chose to be otherwise.

From being a law-abiding physician, he was arrested and unfairly sentenced to a concentration camp in Nazi Germany. There he suffered tragic losses and received inhumane treatment for years. He did survive and wrote a bestselling book explaining how he was able to not only able to survive but learn from his experience. The book is called, "Man's Search for Meaning," and his name is Victor Frankl. While all his basic rights and freedom were taken away, they could not take away his right to choose what kind of person he chose to be. Thus he remained free and this is precisely the point that has application for how you can live. You are a free agent. You may not be able to direct and change so many things but you can choose how you will be and respond accordingly.

For those that believe the person consists of a body, mind, and also spirit, the question of agentic freedom is clear. If the spirit is the enduring component rather than the body then should not the long-term focus then be on the spirit? If so, does the body and mind influence the spirit? From an agentic perspective, it is critically important to ask the question, "Does the spirit influence the body and the mind?" Answering these questions for yourself will be a first step to becoming a better person.

# A Person is a Happening

The belief that body, mind, and spirit are separate entities working in unison has some very practical applications as will be shown in the following story.

*Think of a young mother, we shall call Kindra, who has a wonderful spirit when it comes to loving, helping, and brightening the lives of everyone she touches. However, she just can't find enough time to get a good night's sleep or to take time to eat. She just goes and goes. Yes, everything is working; her mind, her spirit, and her body. Will this last? Of course not, she needs to take better care of herself. While the body, mind, and spirit work together as one, in unity, they each need distinct special care, maintenance, and fuel. It is easier to see the effects of poor maintenance, care, and fueling on the body, but the spirit and mind need equal attention.*

Today, almost everyone agrees that the body and mind are connected. The same is true for those who believe that the body and spirit are inseparable. Combined they are commonly referred to as the soul. But even though these two units are believed to be unitary, coordinate, or inseparable there is no denying that we have separate words for them and they are distinct parts of an enmeshed whole person.

One creative way to answer this mind, body, and spirit question is to say that a person is a not an object but a *happening*. This is not our original idea but a notion borrowed from the existential philosopher, Martin Heideger (1889-1976). He proposed that the unified person is never a static object but something that is continually unfolding and changing. Usually, those who take this position add that the person cannot be separated from the environment and certainly not from others with whom the person is interacting. This notion is especially applicable. Constant change and progression will always be part of understanding a person. Thus there are constant and continuous changes in spirit, body, and mind of the *happening* we call a person.

The important conclusion is that you are more than just a body. Including the spirit when you think and respond to others will result in a richer and more complete way of living.

# Use Many Ways to Find Truth and Knowledge

Like most people, you probably don't spend much time thinking about how you come to know what you believe. We just take it for granted that what we believe must be correct or else we wouldn't believe it in the first place. But how much you trust the different paths to knowing must be considered. So, here is an opportunity to consider just how much you trust the different ways you come to know things.

*Here is an imaginary self employed, self-made father who did not have time for nonsense so he was impatient with his cousin, the magician. Let us drop in on a conversation about what can be trusted. It ended with these remarks:*

*Businessman: It is truly amazing that you could fool my senses like that. Making things appear and disappear right before my eyes.*

*Magician: Actually, such illusions can and do happen all the time. I just stage things to fool the senses of sight, touch, and hearing in order to impress. I don't use my knowledge to deceive.*

*Businessman: But, I could be deceived so easily. I see or should I say, I know that now.*

*Magician: But, if you are aware of the possibility of your senses fooling you, you can then be on guard not to be fooled but still trust your senses because you must use them daily to wisely deal with the world we live in.*

*Businessman: Yes, but my most important problems are about my family. I want certainty. I want what I see or hear to be true. Can I also be deceived there?*

*Magician: Of course. In fact, you have less assurance that what you see and hear when observing people is true. People are much more difficult to observe than physical sight and sounds. Beware!*

*Businessman: So what then?*

*Magician: To be successful , you must see, and hear more than what you observe.*

Rarely are you warned about your senses deceiving you. Instead, you hear the expressions. "Seeing is believing," or "I'd have to hear that from the source." These are two phrases commonly associated with the belief that the most certain knowledge is that which we can hear or see. But, anyone acquainted with philosophy or psychology in the early part of the 20th century knows that what comes to the eye or ear is not what exists in nature. All sensory input is changed, altered, and interpreted by the mind. The popularity and skill of the magician is based on the fact that our senses do not give an exact certain representation of the physical world. Bertrand Russell (1872-1970), philosopher of science, explains that the color, texture, and shape of a table may be very different from what we actually receive thru the senses and yet we always know it to be the same table.

We usually admire the man who says, "Show me or prove it to me first." Prove it, usually means provide evidence that is sensory. And yet, there are many times in our existence where we must act without this kind of knowledge to survive and to prosper. We need to trust others. We need to make conclusions based on reasoning, and circumstantial evidence. We need to be aware that our hard to observe feelings are part of reality. Thus, while a high level of observable objectivity is of great value, it alone cannot answer life's questions about another's spirit, feelings, and emotions. Sometimes we must make subjective judgments in the absence of sensory data. It is necessary to add reasoning; to go beyond what we observe.

# It is Good to be Called Rational but Don't be Satisfied with the Compliment

The following little story will yield light and clarification about the power and limits of reasoning.

*The bright young student: I just detest the debates I have with you. Through your clever, logic you make up seem down, black turns white, and good becomes bad.*

*The professor of logic: Well don't take it so seriously. It is just a game and a good game with rules. I just know how to play it better than you.*

*The bright young student: But it is not a game for me. I want to use my mind to find truth. I want to think clearly. I want to use logic to find truth and to prove it to others.*

*The professor of logic: Well, you might think you are proving something to another if you find them a little less intelligent. Of course, don't plan on really discovering truth with your logic.*

*The bright young student: Why?*

*The professor of logic: Well, the best minds for thousand years have tried and failed. You are really not a good bet if you use reason alone. Don't rely on reason alone to find the final answers to the big questions.*

*The bright young student: So?*

*The professor of logic: Be happy. Be happy you have a good mind, that you can use your thinking skills so well, that you can use these gifts to enhance and improve your personal life. But be humble, for this gift is limited in what it can give to you, and is even more limited in convincing others.*

To understand what this professor is trying to convey, it is important to think about logic logically. It is useful to consider two types of reasoning. The first is reasoning, which has for its basis sensory data. The other kind of reasoning has for its foundation fundamental propositions or premises that are believed to be infallible. Maybe you would call them assumptions. In this case we begin with these acceptable premises, or propositions, then proceed with mental calculations which supposedly guide us to knowledge and truth. It must be obvious to you that the conclusions reached through the most careful and astute reasoning can be no better than the propositions upon which they rest.

In the case of objective reasoning, the conclusions will be wrong if the sensory data was incorrect to start with. As with the other kind of reasoning, the conclusions will be false if the fundamental premise or proposition was in error. For example, if you begin your reasoning with a fundamental belief that people are basically good or people are basically bad, the conclusions reached would be different. Reasoning is a tool used to supplement and expand what may or may not be true beginnings. Furthermore, it can easily be shown, that the mental calculations used in reasoning can lead to inaccurate conclusions through faulty reasoning. Problems in reasoning are easily demonstrated in introductory courses in logic.

Now, realizing that there are problems inherent in both sensory and rational approaches to knowledge, you will still, like most people, use and trust each. So, when you believe that you are a practical person you simply mean that you are capable of employing your senses and reasoning to come to better conclusions. So what if you use both reasoning and sensory observations together, at the same time? This is considered scientific reasoning. Let us discuss scientific reasoning next.

# The Modern World is Built Upon Science That Cannot Know All

The difficulty is that science has proven itself to be the most powerful method of truth finding ever conceived and this may lead some to turn their backs on all the other methods. This will put you at a disadvantage when it comes to understanding people. For now just consider this little introduction between a parent and a psychology professor.

*The psychology professor: So, you would like to know which parenting theory is best.*

*The sincere parent: Yes, not just best but true. Which theory has the most scientific proof?*

*The psychology professor: Actually, you are asking at least three questions: What is best? What is true? What is scientific? I think you will have an answer to all three when you consider that no credible, informed, and honest scientist will claim that his methods can adequately study what cannot be observed or measured. Thus, when you expressed a belief that each person has a spirit and that spirit has something to do with directing behavior, then science is not able to adequately or fully explain what you need to know.*

*The parent interrupts: So I shouldn't turn to science for answers to my parenting questions?*

*The psychology professor: Not quite. Sure you can turn to science for such answers; many will be very good. But don't expect to find a scientific theory that is adequate to explain, predict, or completely inform you with all you want or need to know about parenting.*

*The sincere parent: So, where do I turn?*

*The psychology professor: Turn to science for important information about regularities in behavior, growth patterns, correlations between behaviors and the environment. Science provides many good insights about such matters. But now, knowing this, also realize that in psychology alone there are hundreds of theories. It would be foolish to select one on the basis that it is scientifically true. A genuine scientist will not pretend that he can adequately study the most important aspect of a person, which is the will, soul, spirit, or whatever you call it.*

Again, the greatest and most dramatic illustration of truth finding through the use of sensory information and reasoning is science. Everyone must be impressed with the undeniable achievements of science in the physical world. Scientific disciplines are staffed with men who have proven themselves exceptional in using the scientific method to uncover truth and knowledge.

Thus, without dispute, science is the foundation for truth and knowledge in our technically based society. However, you should be aware that honest scientists will tell you directly that they cannot, and in fact do not want to use this method to tell you about things that are not based on empirical observation. So if you believe that people are more than a material body, then you must turn to other methods for a complete and adequate understanding when dealing with people.

# Give Loving Service First and Then Understand

Here is a story that has taken place many times in many different languages about many different issues. The story will still deliver the same message each time it takes place even though the content and settings change.

*Daughter: Dad said you understand him better than anyone in his life. How do you do that? In fact, you understand me better than anyone else. Mom, what is your secret? Tell me how you do it.*

*Mom: Well, first you should realize that there are many ways and I use them all. But there is one way that is a sure thing; it is by far the best way.*

*Daughter: Well, out with it. Wait a second let me get pencil and paper.*

*Mom: That's not necessary, it is so easy. If I had to use a single word, I would say service; to begin with loving service on a day-to-day basis.*

*Daughter: Do you have a plan and goals when you do this?*

*Mom: Oh, no, nothing like that. It is almost like happiness. If you seek happiness, it eludes you, but if you live right, happiness finds you. So it is with loving service. When you serve another person, you just come to know that person in a way that can't be equaled.*

*Daughter: Yes, I see and maybe that's why so many wives understand their husbands more than they are understood by their husbands.*

*Mom: That's probably a humorous part of the answer. But the principle also seems to work for many men I have met. When they care, help, and see their lives as being in the service of their families, they become men with more understanding. You naturally come to understand the one you serve.*

When students are asked, "Who knows you best?" They do not say, "My therapist." Usually they say, "My mother," secondly, "My father." The mother and father are examples of someone who has served them, shared their life or loved them first. They are not people who are particularly astute in knowing laws and abstractions about human behavior. They are people who have served, lived, and shared a world together. How artificial it is to try and understand someone else in an office. To best understand another person, you need to do things like: eat together, work on a job, share stories, take care of one another when sick, and live with them in a loving, serving, and unselfish way. Does this not tell you about another way to truly understand people, especially those you love most? This conclusion is just the opposite of what we usually think is the way to precede with helping and understanding.

# Experiential Learning Is Not Fully Appreciated

Experiential learning is the basis of what we often refer to as common sense. So, it is important to call this learning to your attention. It should not be overlooked.

*Same daughter: So mother, how much help were those books you read and the classes?*

*Same mother: Of course they helped, but experience or learning from day-to-day activities has proven to be the most valuable kind of learning. Do you think there were no good parents or marriage partners before there were classes and books or understanding others?*

*Daughter: But is this kind of learning as reliable and valid?*

*Mother: Well, thousands each day make life and death decisions based on this kind of knowledge and do so with equal or more confidence than decisions based on academic information. Yes, the answer is a definite yes. I use this knowledge first and even doubt other information if it is not in harmony or consistent with what I know from years of experience.*

*Daughter: Do you think that what you just said is a little self-aggrandizing.*

*Mother: Now that you mention it, I agree, I suppose it is. Sorry but wasn't it you who told me that Dad thought I understood him best. I never found your dad in anything I read young lady!*

There is a kind of knowledge, which comes from experiential living. This is the simple living we all do from infancy to death. We live and interact with people. We learn from meeting them and accepting them in a way in which they become part of our experiential world. Experiential refers to the way that we interpret everyday objects, events, and people as they appear and as they present themselves to us. It truly is informal learning, but perhaps it is the most important type of learning that brings about an understanding of others and our self.

In addition to the direct experiential living that we have, one on one, with the objects of the world and with other people there are our interactions with the knowledge and truth statements that exist in our culture. Here we find information by reading literature, listening from wise people, reflecting and introspecting on our daily observations, paying attention to our traditions, recalling and observing interactions of people with each other, reading, religious practices and instruction, and in all the other ways we learn in our jobs, schools, churches, and private lives.

These interactions and learning gradually accumulate to tell us much about who we are and the people we live with. We come to know individuals directly, but we also acquire certain abstractions and concepts about people in general. Some of us are much better attuned, interested, and intellectually capable of benefiting from this kind of learning, and usually such people share what they have learned. Thus, we learn from one another and from our own experiences a type of truth and knowledge, which is unequaled and irreplaceable for optimal intelligence.

## Life's Meaning Comes From Subjective as Well as Objective Truths

The early existentialists, Martin Heideger (1889-1976) and Soren Kierkegaard (1813-1855) have helped scholars realize that there is a different way to view the world and with a subjective type of knowing that is more fundamental, than a empirical analysis or what Kierkegaard calls objective truth. This experiential type of knowing is for Heidegger, the most important way to find meaning in both material objects and ourselves. So, for students who want, need, and maybe demand an academic base for understanding meaning we will use this insight from existential philosophy. Existentialism is concerned with both the nature of knowing, and also the nature of being a person.

Now, also consider what is probably the most profound statement ever made by a philosopher. It was set forth as the foundation of his work by the father of philosophy, Rene Descartes (1596-1640). He was searching for the one truth about which a person can be absolutely certain. His conclusion was that he knew for certain, that he existed; or in other words, one can be only certain of one's own existence. Thus, his famous statement, "I think, therefore I am." Even a child knows this to be true. First, we accept that we exist, and then we explore what we become.

"Know thyself," "To thine own self be true," "Just be yourself," are a sampling of advice you have undoubtedly heard. Why must you consciously work to accomplish the obvious? Who else could you be, and aren't you always aware of just who you are. Who else would know you better than yourself? For are you not with yourself 24 hours each and every day? Maybe it is easier to understand the popularity of these sayings if you remember the popular phrase, "The unexamined life is not worth living!"

The conclusion to all this is that to be the best possible person, you must know "What are we?" Then, use the most sensible and appropriate methods to understand the illusive and hard to observe spirit of others.  Omitted is an even more important way to respond. It will be discussed next.

# An Appeal to Conscience Is Found In All Cultures In All Times

An artist can draw a picture of the conscience sitting on a woman's shoulder and whispering in her ear. This is a humorous visualization, but let us hope it doesn't trivialize this important resource for acquiring truth and knowledge. Maybe we should worry about the impact of the conversation to follow:

*The postmodernist skeptic: So you claim to be my conscience. Actually, you are nothing more than just an emotional reaction mixed with the things taught while growing up; nothing more.*

*The conscience: Sorry, but let me help you understand that in all these conversations we are having, you are not just you talking to yourself.*

*The postmodernist; Okay, so you exist, but why do some people have you and some don't?*

*The conscience: I'm there for all. I am with all people but well, there is no sense in sticking around if a person won't listen to me. I even leave when a person listens, but consistently chooses to act contrary to what I tell them. Yes, I can see why you would falsely conclude that some people don't have a conscience.*

*The postmodernist: How convenient for you. You disappear when things don't go your way.*

*The conscience: You don't understand my motives. I want to be with each and every person. My motivation is to stay not leave. I'm always available but each person can choose to tune me out. Furthermore, once a person freely chooses to act contrary to what I say, they do not want me to stick around.*

*Postmodernist: Just what I always thought, freedom is more powerful than conscience.*

*Conscience: Yes, but freedom needs conscience more than conscience needs freedom.*

We will later talk about living free and truthful. You may be surprised to learn that living according to your conscience is the only way to truly live free. But before discussing this idea in more depth it is well known that people through all times and places report that they are able to be informed by their conscience. People who receive this type of guidance most often place it above all other forms of knowledge. Some are so trusting and so dedicated to this knowledge, coming from their conscience, that they will forfeit their life rather than to violate their conscience. It is rooted in the deepest of feelings as well as intellect.

The problem with this kind of knowledge is that it does not give the same answers to all people. Everyone seems to have their own conscience and sometimes listening to one's conscience may cause person A to flee and person B to fight. Is there a way to reconcile these opposite responses both based on conscience? If you are to trust your own conscience it would be well to understand these contradictions between what conscience tells different people. Can this problem be resolved?

A most straightforward answer is that what is absolutely right for person A may be absolutely wrong for person B based on differences in the persons, the time, and the circumstances. This is due to context and is not to be confused with relativism. This does not mean that there is no absolute truth and that all is relative to each person's conscience. It means that each person receives an assurance that they are acting according to their conscience even though the answer may not be the same as that received by someone else. This indeed is a complex question. But to live free you must come to terms with your own conscience and decide to trust your conscience. Put conscience in the very center of your decisions. The next story will reveal how to interject conscience to the center of a marriage.

# Your Conscience Is More Than Social Learning

*It was long into the marriage when John discovered that the disputes about right and wrong were misguided activities. When he and Joan decided to change the goal to being good rather than being right, the disputes seemed to evaporate. The advantage in an argument about right or wrong goes to the person who has the best debating skills and is most aggressive in the argument and that was not John.*

*Now after John and his wife stopped approaching their disagreements by trying to determine who was right and instead asked each other, "What is the good thing to do?" things changed dramatically. When searching for what was good, John found he was not at a disadvantage. There was no advantage to the best debater because they appealed to their conscience rather than intellect. Of course, they did not always get the same answer when they listened to their conscience, but it was easier to let go of their own position and consider the answer the other found when searching for what was good. This is hard to do when searching for what is right. Thus, if you believe you have a conscience you might as well use it and if you use your conscience you will come realize how fast many personal disagreements will melt before your eyes when searching for what is the good thing to do.*

Throughout the centuries, references have been made to a conscience. Sometimes it has been called moral sensitivity, an inner knowledge, or a voice that identifies right and wrong, good and bad. In the twentieth century, it has been associated with religion, but even secular humanists refer to conscience as do political and social theorists. It seems to be an accepted distinct and universal attribute. Perhaps some of the more interesting explanations of conscience or something like conscience, has been made by the social biologists. In the writings of E.O. Wilson, the evolutionary biologist, there is an excellent account of how moral sensitivity or altruism has a genetic basis and improves reproductive fitness.

In most cases, the explanations such as those given by the

social biologists and some philosophers refer to something innate and inherited. Conscience is seen as part of the basic makeup of humans. For most social psychologists, conscience refers to learning social norms. But, if you define conscience as simply the learning of social morals and taboos, you probably would have answered this question in the negative because you can dispense with the belief in a conscience and simply explain it as the acquisition of cultural teachings about right and wrong. In philosophical discussions of ethics, something similar to an innate capacity to recognize and know about good and bad, right and wrong is frequently proposed.

So now you see that it is also important that you come to some conclusion about whether you believe you have a conscience. If you do, then conscience will become extremely important for becoming the best possible guide when you face difficult decisions.

# Seek a Meaningful Life and Happiness Will Follow

Everyone will face this motivational question. You have probably guessed by now that these illustrations and examples are given to introduce a new concept. Here is the next story:

*Two beautiful girls graduated from high school and searched for the good life. The responsibilities of parenthood soon fell upon Wilma. The other, named Sue, had a talent for art and design and found she could create, sew, and sell fashionable clothes to fashionable people. While Wilma struggled with a marriage, she dedicated her life to her children and after a second divorce to a second husband, she cared for three children. Meanwhile, Sue had one child, but eventually choose to live unattached by marriage. She associated with a fast crowd having boyfriends, alcohol, and drugs while living in exotic cities.*

*Now they are both old and still good friends. Eventually, Wilma found that family and religion provided meaning for her life. She is the most cheerful person you could meet, filled with gratitude for the love and respect she receives daily from her husband and many children. Sue, however, was motivated more to seek life's pleasures not meaning. Now she has no husband and only a distant son. Her life is hard now and as her beauty slips, she is trying to give up drinking and worries about the lack of sales and the difficulty of sewing with arthritic hands. If you saw them during their early twenties you likely would have concluded that seeking happiness through pleasure was the way to go. Unfortunately, it is hard to see at a young age that you can find pleasure from seeking a meaningful life, but not a meaningful life from seeking pleasure.*

From Freud's pleasure principle to B.F. Skinner's reinforcers the driving force in life is said to be hedonistic personal pleasure. It certainly doesn't require a Ph.D. to know that men like pleasure, and like all animals try to avoid pain. This fundamental truth was known from day one, and requires little time to recognize that each day you spend time trying to do more pleasurable things and want to spend less time doing those things which are troublesome, painful, annoying, and frustrating. This is a true and correct principal. It even could be considered a basic law of human behavior.

But we also know that sometimes we willingly accept a great deal of pain and difficulties to do something that we consider meaningful. One winter you may have shoveled a neighbor's sidewalk because you thought it was a good thing to do. At the onset you knew and later it was confirmed that your face and fingers would become cold. You had discomfort of putting on and off boots, and perhaps you even huffed, puffed, and felt muscle strain while exerting yourself. An athlete in training experiences pain in physical workouts. A father puts up with much unpleasantry working at the butcher shop in order to send his son to college. It is not hard to find examples of meaning trumping pain and pleasure.

Both living to maximize pleasure and living to find meaning in life are true descriptions of the human condition. They are opposites but they both operate in our lives. It is good to live a life with pleasure, even joy, so it is a solid as well as a true principle. The desire to first seek meaning and purpose in life is not meant to destroy or replace the pleasure principle, but it could be seen as a higher law. While both motivations are correct, you must choose for your life whether one or the other is more important. You will eventually choose to guide your life by one or the other.

# Choosing To Be Good Is The Surest Way To Live Free

This concept will be hard to explain, but the following story about a grandfather who lived his whole life on a small homestead in Star Valley, Wyoming is true. Earlier it was mentioned that living true to your conscience is the surest way to live free. This story will be convincing.

*Lorenzo was a poor dairy farmer. With little money and having to milk his cows twice a day, 365 days a year, he hardly had any free time and could not afford to do things that most men would choose to do. It would seem that his poverty robbed him of what many would consider freedom. Yet he was happy, laughed a lot, and had few complaints that could not be handled through humor. He enjoyed the respect of family and friends, and twice a day offered prayers of gratitude to the Lord. He loved his horse, dog, grandchildren, and sons who worked the farm with him. He was known for his honesty kindness, and good nature. By living a good life, by living truthfully, by living true to his conscience could it be said that he was living free?*

In our society, the core question of political, economic, legal and metaphysical philosophy is the question of freedom. It is also an obsession among the general population to be personally free. While this question may not be as important as those presented earlier the freedom question will not go away. So at this time you might want to reexamine the question, "How free am I?"

The question of freedom however, depends on the definition of freedom. Often freedom is associated with the term "agency," referring to the belief that people are free agents. In the usual way of thinking, freedom refers to having the conditions and opportunity to have choices, to say and do as one pleases. Another definition refers to the ability to make choices. A more profound and deep understanding of freedom has to do with how you live. Are some ways of living the key to being free?

In this last way of defining freedom it is how you live that determines your true and honest experience of human freedom. In the simplest terms, it is defining freedom as that state of being that occurs when living a life that is congruent with your true nature or conscience.

## Always Be Changing

Your approach to a human problem might be to have a change of heart or what is sometimes called an awakening of the spirit. This is convincing when reading the case studies in William James's (1842-1910) classic book, "*Varieties of Religious Experience*." William James is known as the father of American psychology, and he reported firsthand accounts of persons who had an awakening of their spirit that was strong enough to immediately and dramatically change their behavior, thinking, and lives. This then leads us to another story.

*Bob was a health enthusiastic and equally dedicated to maintaining his mind. He kept both mind and body in great shape. Bob was rational, analytical, and thoughtful. When relating with his wife he had the energy to give a lot of attention to her. He provided her everything and yet she found their relationship had no zip, zing, or spice. She found him lacking. Realizing this he tried to tell more jokes, to travel to exotic destinations, and meet more friends of her liking. But, nothing he did helped, and though he tried to change, he still remained quite boring and uninteresting. Can he change, should he change, and if so how could it happen?*

Thus, when we consider that all of us are constantly changing it is foolish to fight personal change or try to project an image that we are a finished product. Pretending that we are stable will clash with the truth, and increased unwanted personal instability will be one of the by-products. So let us go to one further application.

## Seek Stability But Love Change

The truth is that we are always changing. Here is a story about stability.

*Susan's father was an alcoholic, her mother neglectful, and she lived in the slums most of her very unstable life. Beautiful and intelligent, she was able to find work and graduate from the university. After a few years, she found herself the mother of three and the wife of a man who had a hard time holding a job and was not physically or socially attractive. She had ample reasons to seek a divorce but never wavered in her devotion, love, and commitment to her husband and children. She was a rock, a rock of stability. With an unstable past, a tumultuous present, and a hard future it is hard to explain why this woman and many like her can be the strength and a stable grounding for their families. Is it that focusing on others rather than self brings stability?*

There is an important, but almost totally overlooked dynamic that helps us understand how we exist. It is the relative strength of the spirit to the body at any moment in time. You can understand this by first noting that the body is constantly changing based on nutrition, energy, rest, stimulation, circumstance, training, etc. The body can be strong, weak, active, and passive while constantly changing.

It is less obvious but equally plausible that the mind and spirit may also have these same characteristics. If so, then what a person is at any moment is a complicated give and take interplay between a dynamic vacillating and changing body, mind, and spirit which all act together as a unity to produce at each moment a person, a different person, and a unique person.

In life we constantly try to find stability; fortunately there is stability. But why are some people more stable than others and to what do you attribute stability? The answer must reflect the extent to which their biochemistry, mind, or spirit give them stability.

To explain how some can be so stable and responsible while

constantly being in a state of change, moving always forward as an unfolding person, is to consider other sources of stability.

Three possible sources of stability are:

1. Being identified or responsible to others.
2. Being connected to God.
3. Living according to your conscience.

Remember these are three ways to be stable as they are related to information that will be discussed later. In the example above, Susan's stability was living in harmony with her conscience. Most likely her conscience would have directed her attention to what she needed to do for others rather than a focus on self. But Susan may also be so identified with her children and husband that she just could not be self-serving. Now, let us turn to a new but related application.

## It Is Not Whether You Will Change But If You Will Change For The Better

It will be an advantage to grasp this simple concept. Of course, one must first accept the belief that change is good.

*Luke was one of those tough self-made men. He came from a disadvantaged childhood and succeeded in school, athletics, and now financially. He was proud of what he had become through his own efforts and owed nobody anything. His new bride adored him and he was confident that he could and would do whatever was required to be successful in maintaining her devotion and love.*

*But life is more powerful than any one man. As a husband it was hard not to ever make mistakes and to be right 100% of the time. Luke began with a positive self-concept, high self-esteem, and an identity as a person who was competent, smart, wise, always virtuous, and never failing. Gradually, he experienced small failures as a grown man with stiff competition. The failures were small and he learned from each but as soon as he had corrected one mistake or weakness, another surfaced.*

*Luke was smart and one day he had a great realization. Instead of becoming stronger, smarter, more athletic, and superior, he was with age actually decreasing in the attributes upon which he had built his self-image. He wasn't even as good looking as he used to be. He was changing and not for the better. Before it was too late, Luke discovered that he could not fight or prevent change. In that very moment his emotions experienced a new freedom and he let go of what he was to accept the challenge and excitement of becoming a new man.*

"He became an entirely different person when he moved to California, "He can't be trusted around her," "He was not that kind of person when he was younger," or "He was never that way with me;". These statements illustrate how people change from time to time and place to place. This belief that people are changing is buttressed by the whole field of developmental psychology. Change in this academic discipline is the one constant in understanding human behavior. It is not a matter of whether we change but how much we change and why, when, and where.

Return for a moment to a previous discussion where we noted that a change in one's bodily state, such as going from sickness to health, or from drug use to sobriety, influences both mind, and/or spirit. There are also some contexts where there are extreme and pronounced effects simultaneously on body, mind, and spirit. The great changes in your identity are those associated with inevitable changes in space and time which are of course part of your life events. Great dramatic changes come from your identification, relationships, and interaction with those intimately loved and God. Religious writings are replete with total transformations seen in the individuals who report that God came into their lives. And the bulk of literature throughout the ages is filled with personal transformation related to loving another. So, it is too easy to answer the question of whether we change, the important question is how much we can change for the better?

## When You Welcome Change, You Can Choose Who You Will Be

It is now a pleasure to propose an action that surely will be considered positive.

*Luke, to whom you have already been introduced, was more than a little resentful that age was forcing him to change. He liked who he was better than the vision of the man he was to be in the future. But Luke was intelligent enough to know that it is fruitless to fight the natural course of life, so he accepted the fact that he was never going to be the man he used to be.*

*The happy part of this seemingly sad story is that there is a happy ending for Luke. It was for Luke a surprisingly happy ending. While he continued going downhill, he found that he was becoming happier. "How could this be?" He thought. "I'm worse but happier." The easiest part to understand about this strange situation was that Luke didn't have to be so perfect; he didn't have to hide or disguise his increasing mistakes and small failures. He even realized that if he ever had a large failure he could even survive that. Actually, it was a little exciting to become a more fallible man not having to be the same super person he was known to be.*

*The best part, however, was the reaction of his wife and children. How could he have known that they actually now liked him more when he was not so perfect? They said he seemed relaxed and was able to laugh more or at least laugh more at himself!*

It might seem paradoxical, but perhaps those who are most satisfied with their present identity are also those who most welcome change in their identity. The truth of this may be seen in the converse where those who have dissatisfaction with their present identity seem to be those who are most defensive and protective of themselves and most fearful of change. However, how much you want to change is an important question for it does have direct applications for what will happen to you in your marriage. If you don't want to change then it is likely that your eventual change will be different than what you want even though you may try to prevent it. But, if you welcome change in your identity, then you can have a more active role in determining the direction and amount of change. Remember, whether you like it or not, you will change.

The essential point of all this is that by welcoming change, you have a better chance in participating and creating your future identity which will, of course, be different anyway than what it is today. These considerations may influence your answer to how much do you welcome, accept, and want personal change.

## People Can Experience Dramatic Change If They First Have a Change of Heart

It would be discouraging if we could only change slowly and in small steps. So here is a good new story.

*There was once a 6 ft. 2 in., 240 lb. young man who was strong, quick, stubborn, and had a temper at times. Some would say he was a little on the rough side as he smoked, occasionally got drunk, and went to parties with a tough crowd.*

*I tell this story because all this stopped. Not gradually but quickly. One day I asked him how, unlike so many others who had a hard time to stop smoking and drinking, he could do it so quickly and completely. I don't recall his exact words but the central point was that he didn't want something like cigarettes or liquor controlling him or his life.*

The majority of experimental research findings in psychology leads to the conclusion that our change or growth is slow and gradual. There are exceptions as observed in the adolescent growth spurt or in the "ah ha" experience in solving a problem. But, the general conclusion based on observations and experiments is that there is gradual improvement as a result of rewarded practice. From B.F. Skinner's theories and research comes the recommended procedure for changing another's behavior. It is to gradually reward successive approximations of the desired behavior. At first, the subject in the experiment or the person in treatment will not be able to make the complete desired response but only can make a small part of the desired action or behavior. Therefore, if they make a small approximation then they should be rewarded and each subsequent reward should be only given when they make a slightly more complete approximation of the desired behavior. This is called shaping and is the recommended procedure for changing behavior. This is not always the way to do things.

In contrast, when one focuses on the spirit of another person the observable behavior and actions become less important. Instead, how the spirit feels or perceives is the critical and most important element. Behavioral change follows a change in the spirit. Fortunately, changes in spirit can occur quickly, dramatically, and completely. A person's behavior changes quickly and markedly to be congruent with the change in the inner spirit. This is the ideal way to bring about rapid change.

There is no disputing the fact that external pressure, rewards, and a combination of carrot and stick can change behavior. The disadvantage is that this behavioral change will usually given grudgingly, slowly, and only enough to gain the rewards or avoid the punishment. When a person's heart is touched, behavioral change will be spontaneous, dramatic and enduring.

## A Stable Identity Is Built Upon Change

Does consistency or does change cause stability? How much are other people a part of my identity? How much do I share an identity with a supreme being? How much does my identity change from time to time and place to place? How much do I want to change?

Existentialists mention a "choosing self," choosing, acting, or living to become just who we are. The existentialist Martin Heidegger refers to this process with the words, "being-in-the-world." Of course, we can't choose, or be whatever we want, for we are certainly limited at least by our body and environment. This is a fact and is called by this philosopher, "facticity." But, at any present moment in time we can, with our facticity, choose to be self-creating beings. We are not an object solely shaped by a determining past. Instead, we are free and choose our future being. The past may inform us about our facticity, but does not determine us or what we become. Life is always moving forward and each person is part of the ever-changing flow forward. So our identity, what we are, is always in a state of forward movement and results from our choices and what we do in the present and not so determined by our past as commonly taught. So now, we come to another application.

## Allowing Others To Be Part Of Our Identity Increases Our Individuality

There is in existential thought or belief that we are not just solitary isolated objects but we exist in relationships with the environment, the culture, and others. Heidegger especially emphasizes that humans, being-in-the-world, are embedded and cannot be extracted from meaningful social interactions. This philosophical concept shows that self-identity must include other people. At the university, most students come seeking to find and wanting to establish their individuality. In marriages, many partners fear they will lose their identity. They are on guard and want to protect their existing individuality. This usually entails making a clear separation of self from other, but with aging we find that this approach is not healthy. The false nature of this beginning is told in the following story:

*Many a young girl like Laura was told during the last years of the 20th century not to depend on someone else, not to sacrifice self for another, to be totally independent, and self-sufficient. This well-meaning advice sounds nice, but there really has never been anyone who has done it, especially in a marriage that was to be happy, and long lasting.*

*Laura was more than just uneasy when heard the words of the marriage ceremony saying to be one, to cleave unto another, and then came a binding ring, a taking on the name of another, the word belonging, and being Mrs. someone else rather than two separate persons. She was even asked by some to put his needs ahead of hers.*

*At age 22, this way of being was a serious problem for Laura, but at age 62, it became laughable. Over the years she learned through family life and love that she lost nothing by being one with the imperfect man she loved, but instead grew to be a more complete person.*

A boat without water is not the same thing as a boat in water. A mother bear with a cub is a different animal than the same mother bear without the cub. The expression "no man is an island" is true when talking about personal identity. So if you want to understand yourself, you must also consider how you define yourself in relationships with significant others. .

A mother is an almost perfect example of this sharing an identity. Even before birth, her baby has become part of her. Her life and identity will from then on never exist apart from her child. A mother and child share, in the course of living, their identity with one another. The mother does not exist separately from the child. This can be true of husband and wife. A consequence or outcome to the first person is a consequence and outcome to the other. Indeed, people who I have a shared identity readily state that when an honor is bestowed on the other, it is as if they had received it themselves, or if the other suffered, they suffered too.

The concept of shared identity may have a very practical meaning for you. Do you find that your identity is closely bound up to the identity of one or more other persons? If so, then to understand yourself you must consider that they are actually part of your identity. Your answer to the above question or concept will open the door for yet another intrusion upon your individuality. This will be discussed next.

# The Most Important Part Of Our Identity Is Already Established

*What if you married a person like Ruth? Ruth is full of expressive love for her God who she literally just worships. She prays in the morning, throughout the day, and at night; always giving thanks and saying, she submits her will to Him. Many a man has married a woman like Ruth. Logically it doesn't look good for the new husband. He certainly will always be in second place and Ruth's husband's will is going to pale in comparison to His will. For Ruth, God will be her head.*

*John thought and worried about this when he married Ruth but found to his surprise that Ruth was a delightful wife. Even though Ruth always saw herself as a child of God, she was equally comfortable being the wife of John. Relating with God adds for Ruth, not diminishes the totality of being a woman. Ruth moved through life being known by her children, friends, and even John as a woman of God. Beginning with her relationship with God, Ruth became a greater person than she could have been alone.*

On the surface, it appears that some think little about God. A supreme being seems to have no part in their life. But that may not be a complete and accurate picture. Is there for all persons a latent concern or awareness of God? Is this activated when extreme circumstances evoke a dormant knowledge? Public opinion polls, survey data, and historic documentation reveal that people have through the centuries and world-wide expressed not only an interest but proclaim a definite and sure knowledge of God.

God is almost always understood in terms of personal lives. The ancient Greeks, for example, prayed, sacrificed, and asked favors of distant, non-loving and not so admirable gods. Relating with God is even more personal with many modern Christians who believe God the Father is a kind heavenly parent who has personal love and concern for each of his children.

In such a case it is easy to see how a God, who is also a father, who is involved daily in one's life, becomes part of a person's identity. The inclusion of God as part of one's identity thus dramatically impacts beliefs, desires, and all that a person thinks about, and certainly the choices made.

If you are a person who believes in God then the understanding of your relationship with God would truly be essential for adequate self-understanding as well as understanding those you love. In such a case God becomes part of your identity that will enhance the meaning and possibilities for making you a better person.

## The Best Answers Are Created For Unique Persons In Unique Circumstances

People like to categorize the world because it helps economize time and effort. If we can put people into classes or groupings then we can treat them according to the classification and life is easier. This approach to understanding people may be attractive, but it has real disadvantages because the action is based on error. To avoid this error, build on the belief that each person is unique and this is good. In the following story, a mother learned to treat each child differently.

*A very religious mother had a problem she could not solve so she turned to prayer to find a way to help her child get over having to have a bottle. An elaborate plan was unfolded and the next day she took the child to a dumpster and told him to throw all the bottles into the dumpster. It was fun. Together they said, "Good-bye bottle." They then went to the store, and as previously discussed, they selected a sack of favorite treats. The next time the child wanted a bottle she just brought out the snack treats and it worked like a charm.*

*Naturally, when the problem came up with her next little boy she did the same routine. Note that she was using the rule or concept that worked so well before, but this little boy was different. He went along just like the first child the first day and had fun throwing the bottles into the dumpster.*

*But later that day when he asked for a bottle and she brought out the sack, he took one look, tossed the whole sack as far as he could, and shouted, "I want my bottle!" For this child, a different answer was needed.*

*Again, the mother turned to prayer and asked why the inspiration that had worked before failed here.*

*The answer: "You didn't ask me what to do for this child."*

When we are analytical, factual, and rational in analyzing a problem, we usually seek to find a principle or a law that regulates whatever we are observing. When the same problem emerges, again we remember the principle and apply it. This makes sense if all people are the same. But each person is unique. Notice that after one century of psychological research, there are not many laws of behavior that have unanimous agreement, or even come close to the consensual agreement similar to these found in the natural and physical sciences. This must tell us something about human individuality.

But another observation is that theoretical laws often do not work because of the unique circumstances that surround each person. Thus, it is more productive to seek ways to understand others in the given situation at the moment. The best answers or solutions are often created in the moment for a special person that is like no other and in a situation that is like no other.

# Behavior Is Caused By Perceptions At The Moment Of Action

This is such a key and important point. The following story and discussion may be helpful to grasp the concept.

*Henry was an embarrassment for his wife at parties. He just acted to impress, grabbing all the attention he could, and worst of all bragging about himself. "Where did he learn to be like this?" she asked. What could she do? Could he be re-socialized in how to act? Could she teach him how to impress the right way? No, that would take forever. He was hopeless. He should have learned basic social skills during his youth and besides how can you teach a person to have social sensibilities anyway? No, the answer is no. He was driving her crazy. When she criticized his bragging, he just got worse.*

*The answer to her predicament came as if in a mental vision. She saw him as a little boy with his male friends each trying to outdo the other with made up achievements. He just wanted to be more important and accepted. Knowing or perceiving this her whole approach changed. Instead of trying to bring him down, to accept that he had a bragging problem, and had nothing to brag about, she instead told him how important he was to her and how she appreciated what he did as a husband. Now that she knew what to do, she didn't worry about how long this was going to take.*

*In social situations, she now saw the same boy trying to impress and she knew that this was no fun for him either and she tried to touch his spirit to give him a feeling of importance. She knew that someday he would find all this bragging unnecessary.*

*Two good things happened. First, she was not so annoyed, and secondly, he gradually changed.*

Even if a person is not totally a product of heredity and environment we will know more about the person if we can learn about the past environment and heredity. Thus, we consider the past to understand the present. But simply understanding the past will not provide the ability to predict future behavior. A better way to understand future behavior is to focus on a person's perceptions at the moment of action. This is the essence of living free. Of course, past experiences do influence the present perceptions, but the word is influence not cause. Another popular alternative in psychology is to say that the past influences present behavior by changing the mind or cognitions of the person.

Present perceptions or cognitions, at the moment of action are among other factors to consider along with the spirit of the person, the situation, and the presence or absence of contributing factors. But, while the past may influence present perceptions, it doesn't cause present perceptions and thus doesn't entirely cause behavior. A more accurate and meaningful way to understand a person is to study how they now perceive the world. If their perceptions are faulty, inaccurate, or in other ways in error, then these perceptions can be influenced for the better but it is not necessary to go back and change the persons past to change present perceptions. We can view others as having free agency then help them have more accurate and honest perceptions.

But even more important than perceptions is the spirit within. It is much more important to discern, feel, and reach another's spirit than intellectually analyze their past if you want a more accurate, honest, and complete understanding.

# Do Not Let Categories Become a Judgement

Carl Rogers and other psychotherapists during the mid 1900's, sought in their psycho therapy to be non-judgmental and accepting. Their emphasis was not on analysis or classification of the client, but on facilitating growth. They believed that by creating a safe, positive, accepting, and therapeutic climate, their client would naturally start moving towards good mental health. They would like this story.

*"I understand you so well." "I've got you figured out," and "I know what kind of person you are," is not what Helen wanted to hear. Yes, she, like most of us, would like to be understood but not this way. She wanted to be understood but not figured out. not analyzed into a type of person. Her husband, similar to so many men, liked to solve problems. The way he solved people problems was to first analyze the person and situation and then determine just what kind of personal classification he could make in order to find a solution. He did this with his wife, Helen. Once he had found the solution, Helen didn't even need to talk any more. Helen understood what was happening with her good intentioned husband and she explained the following to him:*

*Helen: "Jeff, thank you but no thank you for the wonderful analysis. Your effort is appreciated but I just want to run away and scream when someone thinks they have me all figured out. I would hate it even if it were true, but the truth is that I know you error when you put me in a category and predict what I am going to do. That is just not the way people are. I would not do it to you because it is demeaning even if it were possible."*

*Jeff: "So, what do you want?"*

*Helen: "Thanks for asking. When I ask to be understood, I refer to the process of understanding not to a created product called "The Understanding of Helen."'.*

*Jeff: "A process?"*

*Helen: "Yes, an activity where you listen and share my feelings, and try to comprehend what I am going through. It may not need a solution."*

*Jeff: "So, why do it?"*

*Helen: "This is going to take a long time."*

It is very natural when using an analytic technique to try and erect categories, even categories of people, and then to place even our loved ones into these constructed categories. The expected benefit is increased predictability of the other person because we think we know what kind of person is our partner.

There are serious disadvantages to the categorization procedure. Once categorized, the other person has a hard time changing because they tend to believe the category as well. But even if they disbelieve the categorization and do change others find it difficult to accept the change and thus the relationship does not evolve and is stuck where it is.

The way to avoid the problems of categorization is to be non-judgmental in the first place. One of the first benefits is that if you do not judge others they are less likely to judge you. Generally, judgments are judgments of inadequacies rather than of strengths. If one accepts the fact that people are constantly changing then categories become much less useful because people are constantly moving in and out of all of the categories that are constructed.

But, it is not just the accuracy of the judgment that is problematic. It is the judgment itself. The judgment usually is a criticism, and feeling criticism leads to defensiveness, withdrawal, hurt feelings and therefore they typically are detrimental to the relationship. If you can be non-judgmental, non-critical, and come to know others as unique spirits you will find the ways to resolve problems naturally. In time, you can hope to become quite an artist in a way that will be described later.

## It Is Easier To Love When We See an Eternal Spirit

*It was hard for her to know how she could improve her husband, who was clearly in need of help. On one occasion, she was considering a major make over and being a religious woman she decided that her upcoming project needed help from on high. So she turned to God and received quite a surprise. What she heard, to her surprise, was this, "Just focus on you, I'm helping him in my own way." She later reported, "I then saw my husband as a spirit child of God."*

We are distinct and unique because of spirit, body, and mind. But spirit, because it cannot be observed in a pubic and repeated fashion is beyond the ability of scientists to study. But this doesn't mean that your spirit does not exist. It simply means that a psychologist typically would not be able to study you as a unique spirit.

However, behavioral scientists also believe that no two of us are exactly alike, even identical twins. It should be clear at this point that the answers that you gave to the preceding questions now have an important bearing on a choice you can make about whether you believe that you and others are unique spirits. We are kinder, more considerate, patient, forgiving, and understanding when we realize the person standing before us is a unique and eternal spirit.

# Understanding Others Is an Art

*She loved her young son who was quite strong willed for a preschooler. One day, as many children do, he yelled at his mother. Actually the words were "I hate you." Instead of punishing him for disrespect and bad language, the insightful mother had another response. She put her ear on his chest and said, "Let us listen to what your heart says." After listening intensely she kindly looked at him and said she heard his heart say, "I love my mother, but I'm just mad." She did it again, as he held still waiting for another answer, but the same answer came. He was tickled and the whole situation was immediately defused. Then for many times afterwards when this boy made a mistake or had a similar problem, he would turn to his mother and exclaimed," Tell me what my heart says." To both of their delights she put her ear on his chest and she always heard something good.*

The academic disciplines responsible for understanding humans have come to define themselves as a science. This is understandable because science has been so successful in explaining the natural world. If you want to understand self and others in a scientific way, you would either conduct experiments, or draw information from those who have conducted research on human beings. From these experiments, you would, as stated earlier, create the laws that govern behavior. Next, you would apply these laws in a systematic way to yourself, and others whom you have analyzed. You might then say that you approached understanding self and others in a scientific manner, and certainly nothing is wrong in doing this.

On the other hand, the understanding of self and others might better be conceived as an art. If each individual is a unique spirit, the spirit must be considered for an adequate understanding, and science does not offer the requisite information, or at least must offer incomplete information about the spirit. Knowing this, and also knowing that you must come to some understanding of both yourself and others, it would then be wise to obtain information from other sources. To do this you can turn to many other valuable sources of truth and knowledge. Besides gaining outside information, you can come to know the other one through direct face-to-face interactions and experiences.

Thus, as you can see much more is needed to understand a unique changing human being. Subjective judgments must be made, the situation must be considered, and you need to see who this person is, what they are feeling, and respond to the spirit as well as to the body and mind. When using these types of approaches to understand a person and combining them all together, even with scientific principles, you are engaged in a very complicated and creative endeavor. Those that are good at doing this truly are artists. It is not done with a formula but with wisdom, creative insight, and even intuition.

## True Understanding Is Revealed By Both Intellect and Conscience

*Saul had a talent for making good decisions. Around his desk could be found scraps of paper listing the pros and cons in a right or left hand column. Always there were many such pages for each decision. Now, Saul's youngest son caused him to use more and more paper. Over the years, there were many decisions. At first, the questions were simple, like whether money spent on a pet would really help him become a better person. Next, came questions about attending an alternative school, the pro's and con's of a special summer camp, and should he pay for traveling costs in a performing group. Later, the questions were more expensive, like loaning money, maintaining a car, help with taxes, help with a troubled relationship, and the list could continue.*

*These and many, many more decisions were always there and Saul received constant counsel from others that he was producing a spoiled child. Saul listened with interest to the opinions of others repeatedly made his lists of pro and cons and in almost all cases ignored the results of his listings when it came to this son. Instead, he went with his conscience, he went with his heart. In the early years, there was no gratitude shown, and he received little respect from the son. But Saul saw in this son a good person with a kind heart, and his insights could not be calculated intellectually or easily entered into the logical reasoning process that typically guided his decisions year after year.*

*After many years, Saul can now see a young man, working full time, attending the university, and in many other ways being a very responsible person. Saul now knows that he made the right intuitive decisions in the face of contrary advice and reasoning.*

We all need insights to understand other people, and, of course, reasoning or using our intellect is still the traditional and time-honored method used to arrive at insights. However, if one examines the histories of great discoveries in science and in other intellectual endeavors, we find that the greatest discoveries often came in unexpected moments and in ways that were not predicted. Researchers have tried to find the rules that govern the creative discovery and usually find that for the well-trained person, they often have to back away from an exclusive rational approach.

Creative discoveries often come from some kind of subconscious or unexpected, novel, new, visual or auditory experience. Because most of our dealings with people often have a moral component, the insights to understand their moral nature often comes from our moral sensitivity or what we have been calling conscience. The best way to understand and treat another is frequently revealed by our conscience rather than or in addition to a rational, intellectual, or scientific analysis. This concept is very applicable to situations where so many of the difficulties are over moral issues.

## You Can Understand Absolute Truths In The Concrete Situation

*Jon's son had stolen from him repeatedly over the years. Finally, the truth was out and both family and friends said to kick Mick out of the house. This drastic action would help Mick realize the natural consequences of his actions; he was old enough to take care of himself now and Jon could not afford further losses.*

*But Jon did not feel comfortable about this course of action, so he called Mick in to talk it over. The son pleaded to stay, saying it would never happen again. Jon knew his friends were correct in saying that his son would steal again, but something in Jon made him feel that he would take him back in the home anyway. This he did with no uncertainty. He just knew that was what he should do.*

*Well, Jon's family and friends were right, and one year later Jon was faced with the same dishonest actions of the dishonest son. Jon called him in again, but Mick was first to say, "Father, I cannot live here any longer. I am so ashamed of myself. I must move out and I am sorry for disappointing you especially after you gave me a second chance. I don't want to be dishonest and a thief, but until I change I can't face you. Thanks for the second chance." He left without waiting for a reply.*

*Jon now knew, stronger than before and with certainty, he had done right in letting the son stay for the last year.*

If there is nothing other than matter and energy then all truths are simply descriptions of fact. And when it comes to moral statements or statements of ought to, there can be no moral preference, absolutes, or a surety about what is more moral because these are not considered facts. This is the foundation of relativism. And relativism leads to a great deficiency in dealing with the meaningful life.

On the other hand if a spirit exists, if conscience exists, and if a Supreme Being exists, then why not use these sources to know right and wrong, good and bad. What is learned may not be a deduction or application from absolute laws. Instead, it sometimes happens that knowledge is there for the unique individual in a specific context or situation. Thus, one doesn't have to depend on having abstract moral laws to obtain certainty of right or wrong. Instead, one can find right or wrong by using intuition, moral sensitivity, conscience, prayer, and in the broad sense, direct revelation or knowledge. These are associated with the spiritual nature or conscience of a person. It is possible to know what is right, good or desirable in an absolute way, but it is only known in the concrete situation.

# First Understand Another's Heart and Spirit

*Bill knew someone had to help his wife become more social or at least more outgoing and skilled. She in turn thought it was her responsibility to help Bill become more spiritual. Now whether these are desirable and appropriate intentions might be debated, but that is how they felt.*

*Bill was very direct and explained what he was doing as he ordered books and tapes for her instruction. He scheduled social engagements so that she could practice what she learned. Rewards for success were also part of the plan.*

*Now, Rita's plan was based on activities. Church attendance was the foundation, but prayer and scripture study was also an essential element. He could begin immediately and was informed that as progress was made there would be many pleasing surprises in store for him.*

*Both Bill and Rita's plan, as you might imagine, were disasters. The main outcome of each was a giant increase in resentment. Bill, through introspection, determined that unless something was done quickly the resentment would turn into anger and hostility. So he diffused the whole fiasco with humor.*

*Soon both were laughing at the clumsiness and inappropriateness of what they had attempted.*

*After light heartedly reviewing what had transpired, they discussed their desires for one another. Each listened to the other and could see the unselfishness in their failed attempts. Their hearts softened as they laughed at themselves. Then they each said they would try to improve. Bill expressed that he would at least have a positive attitude towards the church and would be open to becoming more religious. Rita expressed that she really was afraid in social situations, but that the goal was beneficial to all concerned. So, she would seek out more positive social experience on her own, with no commitments, and no guarantees. In the few minutes following the laughter more was accomplished than in the weeks spent with Bill and Rita's well-planned programs to change behavior.*

The word "educate" is used because it refers to a broad range of activities to enhance the knowledge, actions, and feeling of another person. It does not refer specifically to teaching. Educate is a highly commendable term, and almost all people must educate in the course of their life. Parents educate, as do teachers, service workers, friends, pastors, and many admirable public servants.

But, the goal of education is all-important. If we educate only for behavioral change much will be lacking. All of us have seen a relationship in which the parties argue to the point that each agrees begrudgingly to change their actions only to satisfy the other person. Clearly, this is an inadequate outcome from a relationship point of view.

A much higher way to educate is to educate the heart or spirit of another person. This usually cannot be done by telling or teaching, but can be done by sharing experiences, setting an example, modeling, and honestly sharing one's confidences and inner feelings in the hopes that the other person's heart will be touched or changed. We often call this a softening of the heart. When a person's spirit or heart is changed, the behavior will follow. We all have experienced a change of heart and know that this kind of change is more meaningful because it is change that can be trusted.

## Rather Than Trying To Make Others More Lovable Become More Loving

*Some would say that Nick was a neat freak but he just wanted to live a well-ordered clean and tidy life. Unfortunately, he married Wanda who proved to be everything he dreamed of, except Wanda was a good-natured slob. She either loved clutter or could not see it. The fact that she continued to buy Knick-Knacks for every room even when they were fully decorated, makes one think she likes to live in clutter. Anyone who walked in their house was overwhelmed with decorating excess. Nick knew what he had to do.*

*The first evidence of Nick's cure was the arrival of a professional decorating magazine. Then he took Wanda to the home of his work associate. the Danish modern home had only three pieces of furniture in each room and each piece seemed to be ankle high, of one color, no accessories, and separated from one another by a shining hardwood floor. The most obvious effort was when Nick told Wanda that his chronic headache went away each time he spent a little time in any sparsely decorated room.*

*All this and much more failed to make any improvements in Wanda's rooms. Finally, Nick exploded in frustration and told Wanda, in no uncertain terms, that the clutter had to go. The clutter did go with Nick and Wanda working together, but the clutter soon came back and quite naturally. Wanda didn't even know how the return came about. This pattern repeated itself so many times that Nick started to think he married the wrong person and now he didn't even have to fake the headaches. He didn't even blink at footing the bill for a marriage counselor.*

*The marriage counselor solved the problem by helping Nick see that he could change Wanda to a tidy, neat, and orderly person, but Wanda would then become irritable, nervous, and unaffectionate. At least this is what Nick thought he heard and this is not what he wanted. He just loved Wanda's sparkling personality and the love she showered upon him. But this was his choice. One year later, everyone noticed that Nick had become just as sloppy as Wanda, and they lived happily and cluttered together.*

Obviously, this little story was just made up to illustrate a point. Most would assume that it is good to help others change but does that mean changing and shaping others the way we think best. There are several professions including teachers, therapists, and social workers whose commendable job is interpreted as changing others for the better but maybe the best way to help others in not to begin with an agenda for changing them.

Perhaps the most beneficial growth and development in another person results from acceptance rather than the intention to change them. This may be so even in a situation where no change is required such as establishing and developing a healthy relationship with another person. The problems that emerge from setting out to intentionally change the other person can be circumvented. In relationships, the healthiest characteristic is accepting and loving the other rather than trying to change someone. In a concrete situation like marriage, rather than trying to change your partner to be more lovable, it is better to change yourself so you can love more.

## Best Experiences Will Be What You Did For Others Not What Others Did For You

*Often it seems like a constant tally is taken to make sure that one person has not done more for the other than they have received from the other. This whole notion of keeping score is turned upside down by the words of this woman written to a newspaper about someone's complaint of a wife "waiting on" her husband. She described herself in this way:*

*"A young couple got married in 1937. Mike worked the third shift for the railroad. He would come in at 7 a.m. to do odd jobs around the house, fix the old car, do everything but go to bed. Finally, about 4 p.m. he'd crawl into the sack, and then it took an atomic bomb to wake him up so he could go to work." Rosie would plead, "Honey, give me your feet, I'll put your socks on for you." "By now it was 1947 and four children later. Rosie never told anyone about how many times she had put on Mike's socks. The number came to about 15,000. Ann, that wife was me. I will soon be 75. Mike has been dead 10 years. I would give anything if I could put on his sock just one more time." Rosie (Ann Landers, June, 1991)*

A wonderful book read by millions is, "*How to Make Friends and Influence People.*" Referring more to the title than the content of this excellent book, it may be better to think: *How to be a Friend and Serve Others*. The way our society is organized requires the service of others in maintaining our automobiles, typing our reports, fixing our appliances, and everything else. We tend to seek service from others and find that the successful person is the one who is able to have others do as much as possible in the way of service for him or her.

Service, however, can be seen as something one can desire to do and one becomes a better person through the performance of service. Thus, giving service to others is to be sought. It is more important to serve others than finding ways to have other serve us through obligation or repayment. If you visit with an old person and they reflect on what were their best years, their best experiences, you will hear not a description of what others did for them but an account of what they did for others.

## Use as Little Power As Possible

*Imagine two men who were married the same day and unknowingly moved into the same neighborhood. They and their brides were about the same age and background. Jake was a strong and powerful man who used a loud voice and definite gestures to communicate what he wanted from his wife and would consistently follow through with ample rewards or negative reactions.*

*Mike on the other hand also had similar expectations but used little social, personal, emotional, of physical power, even in voice or communication, to bring about what he wanted from his wife.*

*You might guess that Jake's wife was a little more on task to say the least. It would seem that Mike would have a little less influence on his wife and success in bringing about what he wanted in marriage.*

*But, when a relationship is evaluated in terms of devotion, dedication, and the feeling of togetherness the results look very different after many years.*

In your opinion would Mike's relationship built on low emotional, persuasive, or physical power prove to be more rewarding and require less effort to maintain in the long run? It just occurred to me that you might even like Mike's approach for the short term. We sometimes describe a person in positive terms as being powerful. These are people who have at their disposal wealth, influence, and other ways to either subtly or directly force others into doing their will.

In relationships, we also see this as a person who is a dominant in the relationship and can use their many powers, including subtle ones of verbal persuasion, and emotion to influence and relate. This individual is often considered the successful person.

A researcher analyzed all the parenting techniques and the outcomes associated with them. A general conclusion emerged. It was that the use of low power by parents was associated with more positive outcomes in children. The reason for this may not be entirely clear, but part of it is due to the better relationships that emerge when the relationship is not based on using power to influence one another.

The successful parents relied on low power methods such as sharing feeling, mutual problem solving, and developing consideration for the wellbeing of the other. This finding will apply to all relationships. So, use as little power as possible.

## It Is Easier To Forgive Big Mistakes Than Little Ones That Come Each Day

*Mary was prepared or at least willing to forgive Ted of potential mistakes because that was the Christ like thing to do for a good Christian woman that she wanted to be. She thought about how she could do this if he were unfaithful, or if he made some other big mistake. After much thought she decided she could. She would forgive him of unfaithfulness or some other equally serious big mistake. But, as we look in on Mary's life, we notice something very contradictory.*

*Mary is a stickler on manners and social graces. Ted falls short here and Mary needs to constantly remind him of his shortcomings in this area, Ted also purchased a boat with money that would have been better spent on carpet and he has never heard the last on it. Ted also accepted a job that later paid much less than expected and Mary constantly reminds him of this mistake. She also cannot tolerate his failures in many other little things. Well, this listing could go on, but you can clearly see that for Mary it is harder to be forgiving of little daily mistakes than the big ones. Well, we may not have to forgive any real big mistakes but the little ones are sure to come.*

Having a long memory is usually seen as an advantage in human relationships. We want to intelligently be aware of past tendencies in the other person so that negative experiences can be avoided or prevented in the future. But if people are to change for the better they need to be believed and accepted in their changed form. Retaining the past is a definite detriment to this. Excellent and scholarly books have been written on the psychological benefits of forgiveness. It seems very clear from the studies that better relationships emerge when there is forgiving of errors.

Change is much more possible and other elements helpful to positive relationships as love and trust emerge when forgiveness, rather than a lasting memory is present.

# When Helping With True Love You Are Freed From Expecting Something In Return

*Like so many, Wendy and Frank began to keep score of who had done what for whom. They used a tit for tat psychological accounting system. This might sound okay and it does work, but it is not good, and here is how Wendy discovered a better way.*

*It was self-discovered and was an accident. Frank came home discouraged and saddened by his performance evaluation at work. She knew about it in a way wives know without their husbands even knowing they had said anything. Even though it was still in the afternoon he fell asleep immediately in a chair and woke up only to begin fixing a broken table he promised to take care of in return for Wendy being so good to him the night before. As he worked, Wendy watched him with compassion and realized that he would tonight take her out to a friend's party that he didn't want to attend because she went to the ball game with him last weekend. She just wished he wouldn't have to keep that agreement too. He worked in silence with a serious expression. He always kept his agreements, he didn't complain, but for the first time she realized he was not happy.*

*She suddenly saw him differently, like she had never seen him; she saw this good, dependable spirit, working hard now and every day. She now wished she could do more for him, even if she didn't have too. She just wanted to help him get over this tough time; she just wanted to help him get over all his rough times. Keeping even or balanced or doing more than her share, or what he could do in return didn't even matter now. From that instant insight or vision she was forever changed.*

Years ago a psychotherapist, Eric Fromm, described two opposite personalities; a manipulative personality vs. a productive personality. He pointed out that in our society the manipulative personality uses others to accomplish his own ends. For the manipulative person, other people are seen as a means to an end; the end being one's own rewards.

The productive personality is a person who tries to produce benefits for all concerned; to self and others. In essence, the productive person is a person who moves ahead by helping others as well as helping oneself. In the life of a productive person helping others facilitates helping oneself, and vice versa.

Perceiving people as more than a material benefactor will move you towards harmonious relationships more than using the other person for one's own ends. If you see someone only as an object, not as a spirit, then it is easy to fall in the mode of using the other person for self-benefit. When this happens, you start keeping score of who has done what for whom. In this way of thinking helping and doing well for the other is required if the other has done an equal amount for you. When this balancing becomes the rule everything changes. Obligation, pay back, making things equal, and being the same, become the goal instead of loving and asking nothing in return. Therefore, when you help another out of love, you are free of needing something in return.

# First Understand the Other's Perspective

*Mary wanted a divorce, which to John was the most foolish thing he could imagine not to mention the usual shock and hurt When first told he blurted out reasons why such a decision would hurt her, hurt him, and be disastrous for the family. The reasons included: financial disadvantages, difficulty of finding another husband, religion, regret, loneliness, and many more. When this didn't change her, he apologized for anything he had done to offend her and said he would fix whatever the problem was. Then he thought that maybe she did not find him romantic or attractive, so he pointed out that she once found him attractive and he would be that same person or whatever she wanted now. You can be sure he ascertained that there was not another man involved. John covered everything when trying to change her mind. Still, she was unmoved.*

*As she went ahead with divorce plans, he presented his case over and over again to her, but he could not understand any of her seemingly shallow answers. He decided she had changed in some significant way and during the next conversation set out to find what had happened. Her health had not changed, to his surprise her values had not either, nor her personality but she did look at things very differently. He listened intently to what she was saying and gradually came to realize that it was not him but marriage that she wanted to leave. The children were gone; she just wanted more out of life than could be found being a wife without children. She wanted to make a difference, to do something to make this a better world, and have a feeling of importance.*

*What a startling discovery for John. He felt an immediate sense of relief and hope. All of what he had been talking about was irrelevant. He knew he could bring her around now that he understood her perspective. He didn't agree or approve of her perspective, but he could live with it and he had full confidence that he could help her stay in the marriage by building on her perspective regarding making a difference and doing her part to make this a better world.*

*We will continue this story later, but for now let us conclude something.*

In relationships we often notice that each party has a point of view and when these are different the relationship suffers, and when they become more similar the relationship seems to run smoothly. In the case of conflicting perspectives, the common solution is to get the other person to view things the way we do. This is beneficial to the relationship, but is usually done at great costs and difficulty because typically the other person resists, counters, argues, and tries to maintain their own position.

## Don't Feel Sorry For The One Who Is Loved Less But Loves More

*When John pointed out that Mary could follow her dream within their marriage she dropped her plans for divorce. As you might have predicted, the marriage was just not the same. As the years dragged on Mary became increasingly preoccupied with causes, action groups, and community affairs. She seemed to be always disappointed in the progress, and never had enough time as she moved from one engagement to another.*

*John supported her but felt left out. She urged him to participate but he missed the time they spent alone together. He felt he was an afterthought or put second to every one of the programs that so occupied her time. Sometimes he thought that he shouldn't have talked her into staying in the marriage. Maybe he should now get a divorce but he couldn't; he just loved her too much. No, he would just love her, help her, and make life as good as he could for both of them.*

*As the years went by he was able to do a better and better job of making life enjoyable for each. So what if he was second place, he was happy. At least it wasn't second place to another man. He even learned how to cheer her up or to divert her attention when she was moody from things so often not going the way she wanted. He was always there, smiling, cheerful, and happy and that is what she was able to notice late one afternoon. She realized, just in time, that he was happy and she was not.*

In some strange way we are lead to believe that when one person loves another more than they are loved back that they suffer. The opposite is true. To love another more has its own reward. To love another less moves one away from the happiness that is available. So don't feel sorry for the one who is loved less but loves more.

# The Good Thing To Do Theory

*"My husband and I are from different cultures and countries. We have to handle problems in a different way so we both feel like the problems are being resolved without hurting the other. Understanding comes first and it comes from love, acceptance, freedom, and respect, because if we have all these things in mind it will be easy to resolve the problems and love our partner more every day."*

All the information presented thus far can move us to use a very simple, but useful mini theory. This little theory is associated with a radical idea. The idea is that each person should construct a special way to respond towards every other unique individual in their life. Thus, there should be as many theories as there are people. Accordingly, we need to create our own theory for each person because each person is unique; like no other. This requires a significant change in thinking about self and others. For the material world of matter and energy the hope is to discover a single theory that yields the true general laws of behavior that then apply to all people. When it comes to understanding matter and energy this has been the most useful approach.

This approach is still helpful, but will not do the job. Each person is not only unique but is also constantly changing. A person will not stay the same person. Thus, we soon find that successful understanding of self and others becomes an art. It is an art wherein you must adapt your understanding moment by moment as the person in front of you changes; becoming softer, harder, more fragile, stronger, etc. Emotions go up, and then down and attention shifts. Understanding then requires that as you change you interpret what the other is saying and feeling. Thus the unique theory for each individual must also change moment to moment. Therefore, only the skillful artist can maintain understanding and respond to the other with continuing intelligence.

The goal is not to classify or categorize the other or yourself. The goal is to give or respond with love and understanding. It is to help the other see and perceive the world more accurately. It is to facilitate the inner positive growth force that will help the other person become a better person. What to do is typically not known in advance but emerges spontaneously in the interactions and conversations between two people.

It happens when there is genuine respect, love, freedom, and acceptance in the relationship.

The new way or theory has the following characteristics:

1. A unique theory is created for each person.
2. The unique theory needs to constantly change from moment to moment.
3. Creating the theory is an art.
4. Understanding comes from loving, acceptance, freedom, and respect.
5. Understanding another requires a changing self.

These five listings are based on statements that have already been presented. You need not agree with all of the earlier statements, but hopefully, there was enough agreement so that the above five statements are acceptable to you, even desirable.

Another consideration follows when you already have a strong belief in the existence of the spirit and of conscience. Actually, if we believe the survey data available most people, including university students, believe in spirituality. As already discussed, a belief in spirituality provides a very different way to view and respond to the other person who is a spirit and can be informed by a conscience. In this view we are much more than conditioned animals of material substance. Flowing from both existential and Christian thought this mini theory provides a fuller view of man when it is held that:

1. A person, being spiritual, can experience dramatic change.
2. A person, being spiritual, can come to truth and knowledge in many ways.

While the exact relationship between the body, mind, and spirit is not completely understood this better way mini theory helps us to not overlook the most important and enduring part of being human. The seven basics listed above lead to the conclusion that we need to relate with other people in a way that has the following elements: love, service, forgiveness, and acceptance in a non-judgmental way. The belief that man is basically good or a child of God leads us to being a helping person who does not believe that power or coercion is required to make people be good. Instead, the approach should be based on practices that free a person to live according to a natural desire to be good.

Thus, these elements could be called the: *"What Is the Good Thing to Do Theory."* This theory flows naturally from our heritage and beliefs. It was not necessary to bring in the existentialists, but it may please scholarly students and associates. Nevertheless, this *"What Is the Good Thing to Do Theory,"* provides a simple way to make decisions.

You may have noticed that the choices you were asked to make during the reading of this book became more and more specific as you read. Choices became very specific and actually came to deal with what is the good thing to do. This is the main objective. All the questions and choices are meant to help you become your best possible person.

There emerged many insights but being a good person is the key. In order to be more precise about being good, consider these practical clarifications about choosing to be good that follow from the *"**What Is the Good Thing to Do Theory?**"*

1. Being Good is both a choice and an action.
2. Being Good is within the ability of all to understand.
3. Being Good is the natural you.
4. Being Good is known at the moment of action.
5. Being Good is a joyful and desirable feeling.
6. Being Good is being loving.
7. Being Good is being responsible.
8. Being Good is being honest and truthful.
9. Being Good is being unselfish, putting others ahead of self.

10. Being Good is being non-judgmental.

11. Being Good is being forgiving.

12. Being Good is being devoted, loyal, dependable and committed.

A student from the class, commented;

*"The last lecture says it all. I like the basic question, "What is the good thing for me to do?" This question is perfect. If I was to ask this every time before making a decision in my life. I believe that my wife is good at doing this. She is able to step back from a situation and think, what is the good thing to do. When she does this she then approaches me with a gentle and loving attitude and desire to peacefully work out any miscommunication or disagreement.*

Again, all your answers and choices lead now to one easy to remember conclusion, which by itself is the best way to be. It is to always be asking:

**"What is the good thing for me to do?"**

Nothing else, nothing you can learn, nothing you can change in your life will be as important. Everything you have read supports this single conclusion. Even if you have forgotten half of what you read the residue and lingering impressions that you are a unique spirit, have a conscience, are constantly changing, are free, have many ways of knowing, etc., are enough to awaken in you the awareness that you are a good person. You are a good person to start with and it is your natural way to be and live. You need not be a totally good person, but by asking the question above, you will always be moving in the right direction. How does this happen? Here again is the simple and easy way. It is to ask:

**"What is the good thing for me to do?"**

If you ask this sincerely, the answers will come. And the answer you receive will always be growth promoting and the best guide at each moment. Other ways to live are shallow when compared with always choosing to do what is good. If you are a religious person, you can ask the same question using different words. They are:

*"What would God have me do?"*

The results and processes are the same. You will know what to do and it will be what is best for you at that moment.

As the class came to a close a self-test was administered to the class. You might enjoy comparing your thoughts and feelings with the class. At the bottom of the self-test are the most common ratings from the class. You can take the self-test and compare your results against the class results.

# SELF TEST

Circle one of the following numbers that best describes your feeling.

1.    The most important part of me is my spirit rather than my mind or body.

| Strongly Agree | Agree | Undecided | Disagree | Strongly Disagree |
|---|---|---|---|---|
| 1 | 2 | 3 | 4 | 5 |

2.    I am not just the product of heredity and environment, but can choose what I will be and do.

| Strongly Agree | Agree | Undecided | Disagree | Strongly Disagree |
|---|---|---|---|---|
| 1 | 2 | 3 | 4 | 5 |

3.    I welcome, seek, personal change each day.

| Strongly Agree | Agree | Undecided | Disagree | Strongly Disagree |
|---|---|---|---|---|
| 1 | 2 | 3 | 4 | 5 |

4.    My conscience is important for finding truth and knowledge each day.

| Strongly Agree | Agree | Undecided | Disagree | Strongly Disagree |
|---|---|---|---|---|
| 1 | 2 | 3 | 4 | 5 |

4.    My conscience is important for finding truth and knowledge each day.

| Strongly Agree | Agree | Undecided | Disagree | Strongly Disagree |
|---|---|---|---|---|
| 1 | 2 | 3 | 4 | 5 |

5.    It is more important to find unique answer's for unique personalities than to find general rules.

| Strongly Agree | Agree | Undecided | Disagree | Strongly Disagree |
|---|---|---|---|---|
| 1 | 2 | 3 | 4 | 5 |

6.    I am not afraid but desire to share an identity with others.

| Strongly Agree | Agree | Undecided | Disagree | Strongly Disagree |
|---|---|---|---|---|
| 1 | 2 | 3 | 4 | 5 |

7.     The most important thing I can do is for me to become a better person.

| Strongly Agree | Agree | Undecided | Disagree | Strongly Disagree |
|---|---|---|---|---|
| 1 | 2 | 3 | 4 | 5 |

8.     It is more important to change our hearts and spirit than to change behavior.

| Strongly Agree | Agree | Undecided | Disagree | Strongly Disagree |
|---|---|---|---|---|
| 1 | 2 | 3 | 4 | 5 |

9.     It is more important to ask, "What is the good thing to do" than "What is fair," "What is reasonable," or "What is practical."

| Strongly Agree | Agree | Undecided | Disagree | Strongly Disagree |
|---|---|---|---|---|
| 1 | 2 | 3 | 4 | 5 |

10.     Asking, "What is the good thing to do" is like asking, "What would God have me do."

| Strongly Agree | Agree | Undecided | Disagree | Strongly Disagree |
|---|---|---|---|---|
| 1 | 2 | 3 | 4 | 5 |

11.     It is possible to directly know, "What is the good thing to do" and "What would God have me do."

| Strongly Agree | Agree | Undecided | Disagree | Strongly Disagree |
|---|---|---|---|---|
| 1 | 2 | 3 | 4 | 5 |

# MOST COMMON RESPONSE OF CLASS
# TO EACH QUESTION:

1. Strongly Agree
2. Strongly Agree
3. Agree
4. Agree
5. Strongly Agree
6. Agree
7. Strongly Agree
8. Strongly Agree
9. Agree
10. Strongly Agree
11. Strongly Agree

# ABOUT PROFESSOR JENSEN

Professor Jensen was born in 1938 and grew up in Wyoming, Montana, and Colorado. He is married to Janet Mitchell and is father to 10 children, 33 grandchildren, and 3 great grandchildren.

After graduating from Wheat Ridge High School in Colorado he received B.S. and M.S. Degrees from Brigham Young University and his Ph.D. degree from Michigan State University.

Professor Jensen has taught at the following universities:

1. Michigan State University
2. State University of New York at Potsdam
3. Brigham Young University at Provo
4. Brigham Young University at Hawaii
5. Utah State University
6. Southern Virginia University

He has consulted for:

1. Research for Better Schools
2. Journal of Child Development
3. Psychological Reports and Perceptual Motor Skills
4. Family Research Center Brigham Young University
5. Provo and Salt Lake City Public Schools
6. Institute for Population Studies in Exeter England

His books include the following:

1. What's Right What's Wrong
2. Understanding and Using Social Influence Techniques
3. That's Not Fair
4. Moral Reasoning: A Philosophical and Psychological Intergration

5. Responsibility and Morality

6. Feelings: Helping Children Understand Emotions

7. History of Moral Education

8. Stepping Into Step-Parenting

9. Adolescence

10. Parenting: An Applied Textbook

11. Family Feminism

12. Families: The Key to a Prosperous and Compassionate Society in the 21st Century

He has published over 100 scholarly articles in scientific journals.